Reflections

Of

Him

Let His Love toward all the problems facing you today and in the future

By Barbara DeCroix

Barbara DeCroix

Library of Congress Cataloging in Publications Data

DeCroix, Barbara

Reflections of Him

ISBN – 9781794477100

Manufactured in USA

First Edition

Cover created from a photo by Barbara Decroix

Copies of this book may be ordered from https://www.amazon.com/s?k=reflections+of+him&ref=nb_sb_noss_1

DEDICATION

This book is dedicated to Him who is the Author and Finisher of our faith!! So many times we run aground but He is always faithful!!

FOREWORD

In the passing decades, some of us become increasingly aware of the unique stamp of God on each and every human being. As no two fingerprints are exactly alike, so no two individuals are the same. This is true with the application and expression of God's special gifting to men and women. The New Testament teaches that all Christian believers are endowed with spiritual enablements. Barbara, whom I have had the pleasure of knowing for several years now, originally meeting her on my vacation in southwest Florida, has certainly and delightfully proven this to be unquestionably so. She has what I would call a "spiritual-poetical" gifting of sorts. Along with her long-standing ministry and love for the hearing-impaired, she displays a unique ability to sense the spiritual in the natural world.

Barb, in my hopefully circumspect judgement, has been graced with uncanny "flashings" and "onrushes" of spiritual perceptivity, which are sometimes presented in forthright fashion. More than one time I have found her penetrating remarks thought-provoking, whereas afterward I could only pause in silence. Her insights are typically expressed informally in Christian conversation and, on occasion, formally in verse. In some sense she bears the truth of what the Apostle Paul, teaching in his second letter to the Corinthian church, chapter 3 verse 18-"And we all, with unveiled face, beholding/reflecting the glory of the Lord, are being transformed..."

As you thoughtfully read "Reflections of Him," you will find yourself staring into the mirror of her soul as she views and reflects back revelations from on high. May God talk to YOU through her vivid poetry and meditations, and may Jesus Christ be glorified.

Pastor Robert Harrell

INTRODUCTION

This book has taken 15 years to write. I heard a very wise man, Judson Cornwall, expound on the value of journaling your thoughts and prayers so that you could go back and read them over and, as I obeyed, I was surprised what else the Lord had to show me. I started journaling and the result....Reflections of Him. I urge you, no matter where your journey takes you, to keep a running tablet of your walk with Christ!! I hope that you will thoughtfully and prayerfully read these verses and allow the Lord to touch you as He has me!! What a Great and Wonderful Friend we have in HIM!!

REFLECTIONS OF HIM

POETRY

REFLECTIONS

A chorus of rainbows

Bright flowers in a vase

All are but a picture

Reflections of Thy Grace.

A tapestry of life's events

Winding down an unseen road

Peaks and valleys, highs and lows

But perfection, yes perfection, being told.

After all these years yet the quest remains

Bond-Slave or servant still?

Heavenly Father only you know my heart

Bring to fruition Thy Will.

JESUS

I know a Man, a special Man
Who came from Galilee
One touch and the lame do walk
One sigh and the blind do see.

I know a Savior, a special Savior
Born to taste my punishment
On His Cross, He forgave us all
Bowed His head and the veil was rent.

I know a Friend, a special Friend
Who calms my troubled seas
He spoke not a word but shed His Blood
For a sinner such as me.

I know a King, a special King
Clothed with humility
Love is His scepter, grace His crown
Peace His battle-theme.

I know a Love, a special Love
I will live eternally
Mansions on golden streets are prepared
But His dear Face I'll see.

Jesus means all this to me and I hope to you too.
If not, bow your head and open you heart, ask Him in
and He will fellowship with you too.

THE QUESTION

How would you answer?
What would you say?
If I required an account of Yesterday?
How many people have been saved
By the testimony of My Word that you gave?
How many Amens have been left unsaid,
Boasting of mans frailties and not my Son instead?
Yes, how would you answer?
What would you say?
If I required an account of Yesterday?

How would you answer?
What would you say?
If I required an account of Today?
Would you be found praising My Name?
Or sitting in front of the TV watching the game?
How many scriptures have been read,
Filling your soul with My Love, and not
the world's dread?
Yes how would you answer? What would you say,
If I required an account of
Today?

How would you answer on the Morrow
If I required your soul Tomorrow?
Would you stand in my
Presence in sins nakedness,
Or be fully clothed in My Righteousness?

If I asked you to search the Lambs book,
Would you find your name if you looked?
How would you answer on the Morrow,
If I required your soul Tomorrow?

These are open-ended questions
But how important are the answers?
They define your future
Heavens love song or Hells deadly cancer.
So ...how do you answer?
What ... do ... you ...say?

BABE

He was born in a stable
He lay on the hay
He was pure but was able
To make angels sway.

A star shone atop the stable that night
To lead the Wise Men with its shining light
They brought precious gifts of
silver and gold
To lay at His feet for the world to behold.

The shepherds with their flocks did bring
Adoration and worship
To the Babe their King.

What did this Babe have to bring?
Was it money? Riches?
No none of those things.
What He brought was a Gift from above.
A gift of His Life and His Fathers Great Love.

So at this Christmas time
Stop and pray
And give yourself anew to the Babe today!!

NOTES

How has the Lord reflected Himself through these verses?

1.

2.

A BLESSING

He always gives us Blessings
In His Own special way.
Always guiding and protecting
During the storms of life each day.

His Word is always waiting
For a hungry soul to feed
His Love cannot be separated
From those who choose to believe.

His Arms of Comfort and Mercy
Are always open wide
For those who have gone the sinner's road
He will gently pull them to His Side.

His Ears are always listening
For the humble, silent plea
Forgiving and forgetting is to
Him His humble deed.

His Name is above all other names
Excellence in virtue, humble in Heart
Willing to give His Life for all
Yes, a true Blessing set apart.

HEAVEN

When the veil of death is lifted
And we can clearly see
The Wonders of His Perfect Love
T'will brings sinners to their knees.

The rainbows of the heavens
Trees of multi-colored leaves
Grass so rich and fertile
Oh, the everlasting peace!!

The joys of life eternal
No more pangs of pain
Only eons of happiness
Will be our future fame.

No more darkness, no more doubts
No more questioning
No more fears to confound us
Only His Face we'll see.

All this because He did devote
His Blessed Sacred Head
His Heart of Love spilled out for us
In the rich color of His death.

Come one, come all
To this Blessed Grace
Pilgrims, Sojourners, Wandering Ones
Humble your heart, to His Embrace!!

HIS

His Grace put the petals on
the flower
His Grace dressed the trees
in green
His Grace put a song in the bird's mouth
His Grace hung on a cross for me.

His Mercy turned the blossom
to face the sun.
His Mercy caused the cascading
green to shade.
His Mercy put the warble in the bird's song
His Mercy hung on a cross for me.

His Love caused the flower's seed to
fertilize the soil
His Love called the weary traveler to sit
'neath the shade
His Love taught the bird to call for his mate.
His Love hung on the cross for me.!!

NOTES

How has the Lord reflected Himself through these verses?

1.

2.

HIS GRACE

I can look at the cross

Where Your Body was laid

But I can never understand

The Price that you paid

For my grace that is so rich and free

All because the law exacted its penalty from Thee!

I can look at the grave with Thy Body within

But I will never quite understand

The penalty for my sins

Your Love is so true and beyond compare

It hides all the darkness of the sin You did bear.

My heart sings a plaintive melody

Knowing my chains were broken thru thy Suffering

If only there was a way to repay …

"Oh, but there is", says my soul

ONLY OBEY!!

HIS PRESENCE
(1970)

We all stand before God naked
Stripped of all our clothes
Our souls are barren in His sight
Why? This is the way He chose.

We are not to question our Father
Don't ask why, where or when
He has reasons that will better our lives
Though we couldn't see it just then.

He has ordained our life and
He also knows the end
We couldn't understand the trials
No, not just then.

So pray to the Father
And in faith look to the Rock
Knowing that when the darkness lifts
There will be no need of clocks!!

HIS SIGNATURE

I hear a bird calling to his mate

A song only You could create.

I see a bell hanging from a tree

Ringing and calling together families.

I feel a flutter against my cheek

It is your Presence that I seek!!

Out of the corner of my soul's eye

Is that the finish line I spy?

Excitement and doubt course up my spine

It won't be long till I am with My Savior Divine

Will He say the words I am longing to hear,

"Faithful servant your REST is here."

Please make my senses attentive I pray

To the sounds of Your Signature each day

And I will humbly praise Thy Name

As I journey through life's waiting game.

NOTES

How has the Lord reflected Himself through these verses?

1.

2.

ALONE

Sitting alone at the table

Listening to the swirling sounds

Everything seems so chaotic

Yet there is no one around.

Is that *my* soul I am hearing?

Are these *my* mindless thoughts?

Is this *my* life in a frenzy?

Oh what sins folly I bought!

I believed the world and its promises

I followed my feelings not faith

Presumption and lies nipped at my heart

Ruin and destruction I faced!

Then His Blood-Stained fingers dried my tears

His Mercy covered my sorrows

His Crown of Thorns purchased my fears and

His Love bought all my TOMORROWS!!

GOD IS THERE

When you hunger for things that can't satisfy

When you thirst for things without substance

When you need a blanket to stave off the cold

GOD IS THERE!!

When your heart has been broken in a million pieces

And you don't think things will ever be the same

When you cry out but nobody hears you, nobody calls
your name

GOD IS THERE!!

When darkness is all around you and

gloom starts to settle

When there is nothing left to pursue or to seek

When you're loved one has taken his FINAL journey

You feel so alone and weak

GOD IS THERE!!

No matter the situation or frame of time

God has created a safe place to fall Into

His Love Divine!!

LIGHT   (1972)

Keep your eyes above that way

they won't look down

Keep your eyes above, keep them

off the ground.

Keep your eyes above let them

see the Shining Light.

Let the Lord be your Guide. Let the

Lord be your Guide.

When everything else crumbles the Lord
will be your Guide.

Let the Lord be your eyes

Let the Lord be your ears

Let the Lord be the center and core
of all your years.

NOTES

How has the Lord reflected Himself through these verses?

1.

2.

LOVE IS CALLING

Love called my name
But I ignored it
Love called my name
But I withdrew
Love called my name
But I pretended not to listen
Yet Love remained True!

Your Love depends not on my answer
Your Love is True where all else is false
Your Love is the Gateway to Life Eternal;
Your Love is Truth at any cost!

My ears and eyes so deaf and blind
Have opened to Thy Plea
I hear Love's Voice calling
Thank you for remembering me.

To others who may have lost their way
Or been blinded by their sin
There is still a Love Voice calling
"Return, Return to HIM."

LOVE LETTER

My body became the parchment

Sneers and Jabs became a way of life

Scourgings and beatings became harsh

bedfellows

But I silently surrendered to the strife.

The letter had to be written

Our purpose was very real.

On a lonely hill the letter was sent

With My Blood as its Seal.

All honor to the Father

All praise to the Son

Who willingly surrendered

That our hearts, to the Father, could be ONE.

MY PRAYER

Don't allow me to sing a song about You

Allow me to become the song You sing.

Don't allow me to preach a message about You

Allow me to become the message

that You preach.

Don't allow the Holy Spirit to just ruffle my hair

Allow Him to breathe in and through me to help
others.

Don't allow the world and its pleasures to
consume me

Rather help me to consume the world and its
pleasures

With Your Love.

If I only do for You, I will be emptied at some point

But if I allow Your Character to dwell in me,

I will have Your Presence with me always.

NOTES

How has the Lord reflected Himself through these verses?

1.

2.

MOUNTAINS

If I could climb a mountain

Would I see Thy Very Face?

If I could shinny up a tree

Would I feel Thy Strong Embrace?

If you could climb a mountain, child,

You would *Not* see my face

If you could shinny up a tree

You would not feel My Strong Embrace.

But, if that is your desire

What you truly want to see

Go to 22nd street and feed the hungry

Give your coat to someone cold,

Tie the shoe of the arthritic and old.

When you look upon them you shall see My Face

When they give you hugs of thanks,

You shall feel My Strong Embrace!!

THE REED

(Written by Robert Harrell)

A reed in the breeze
The older man sees
"What is my life but a bending of reeds.
There is no calm tomorrow. No chanceless
estate
Untouched by the current of merciless fate.

"Ah".......thought He twice, "There's more to
be seen
Like the space in the grass
A truth in-between."

   The Source of that Wind!
   The Start of that Swirl
   The Fount of that gust
   The cause of that whirl!

For God is the root of the reed and the blow
In this I obey for this Truth I know.
He deems that I bend and sway with the air
Along with the flurry

   Yet without care!!

REST

I looked at the world and I did sigh
From deep within came this cry
"Is there no rest for my soul?

Is there nowhere for me to hide?
Nowhere for me to abide?
The pressures come they will not cease
I cannot seem to find relief
"Is there no rest for my soul?"

Are there no gardens green?
No waters full?
No place to lay my head until
This nightmare is past and
The storm is stilled.
"Is there no rest for my soul?"

I heard a voice and looked up high
From heaven this word came nigh:

"Yes there is rest for thy soul
In My Nail-Pierced Hands you can hide
Under my Wing you can safely abide
The world's pressures find no pleasure in Me
So under My Banner is complete security.
Yes there is rest, sweet rest for thy soul!!"

NOTES

How has the Lord reflected Himself through these verses?

1.

2.

SIMPLICITY

The hardest thing today to see
Is that God, is in all SIMPLICITY.
I said "How could a God like He
Love someone as insignificant as me?"
His answer was "Very easily.
All I ask is that you choose me
And be in love and obedience faithfully."
Then in my darkness a light did shine
For I knew the Love of God was mine.

I will fail Him every day but
He picks me up and leads my way.
The perfectness that I once sought
Has already been bought with the
Precious Blood of His Beloved Son.
My God and I can now be one.

I worked so hard to deserve His Love
And now I know it comes from above
That fateful day on Calvary
My Jesus died in Love for me. So
In myself is no righteousness.
My Lord and My God is the Giver of this.

I thank my God for giving to me
The gift of His Love and His Security!!

SUCCESSFUL FAILURE

I had everything life could afford

I had it all but still I was bored.

The statues to my successes had all turned to rust,

while my spirit and soul had remained UNTOUCHED

I meditate again, how could I have thought

Those foolish things could buy what I sought

Success, fame, yes, but at what a high cost

My values, my peace, myself I have lost!!

The thing I believed would lead me to bliss

Has all turned into a big NOTHINGNESS

And I stand now looking at the ruin of a man

Who thought he had everything, his future planned!

If there is a way out, an escape for me

Please enlighten before I walk into eternity.

Be willing to show me the way

Without your help, I will just fade away.

SUCCESS

How would you define success?

Is it the one with the most business sense?

Or is it tied to a monetary measure?

Maybe a big home or a fancy car is its
treasure?

Or is it more self-contained

Inside the heart of a human frame

Maybe a tender word softly spoken

Healing a heart just recently broken?

Or is it that smile on your face

That leads me to a peaceful place

Where I can be myself and not fret?

Yes, I guess that is SUCCESS

NOTES

How has the Lord reflected Himself through these verses?

    1.

    2.

MEMORIAL AT SANDY HOOK

The morning air was crisp and clear
As Connecticut mothers were saying
"Wake up dears".
Complaining children arose from their beds
Ate their last breakfast
Not knowing the future ahead.

The angels were crying, I know it did rain
For the 26 that were then slain.
At the same moment a party erupted
For those who had just been transported.

Heavenly portals opened wide
To usher 26 new angels inside.
Little eyes opened wide
When they saw the gifts inside.

Gifts of joy and of peace
Not one frown?
Oh, look on cloud #7
A campground of clowns.

As another door opened
You could hear shouts of glee
"My favorite toys …
And they are all FREE."

The music was rapturous
Not a note off-key
As the new recruits joined
and sang endlessly.

The horrific tragedy that happened on earth
Has become heaven's blessings,
26 new souls birthed.

IN HONOR OF HANK (MY HUSBAND)

A Garden...warmed by the Son

A Garden...watered with His Tears

A Garden... planted by His Loving Hands

A Flower is Born.

The flower turned its face towards the Son

The stalk held its beauty for all to see

The essence of its perfume filled the air

The Flower Grew.

The flower cut at its stalk

Its perfume wafted towards the heavens

Another flower was added that day

To His Bouquet of Love!

NOTES

How has the Lord reflected Himself through these verses?

1.

2.

DON'T TAKE YOURSELF SO SERIOUSLY
(Inspired by Donna, age 105)

My clothes are dirty and spotted again
My shoes are full of mud
My car needs a wash, the bikes tires are flat
But I myself am laughing at that.

Years ago, that would have put me in a din
My eyes would bulge out, my voice sound like tin
Nothing would have given me any pleasure
Until all the mess was over.

You may ask, "Change of attitude?"
"Time heals all wounds" is the right platitude.
So if you want to live a life stress free
Just don't take yourself so seriously.

My faucet drips
My showerhead leaks
On top of that
My floors creak!!

Oh no, I feel a spin coming on,
My eyes are bulging out, my voice going down
Nothing will give me any pleasure
Till all this mess is over.

You may ask "change of attitude?"
"Time heals all wounds" is the wrong platitude.
Suck it up and live out your rhyme
Don't take yourself so seriously next time.

My eyes shutter against the light
Beads of sweat do appear
My teeth are clenched tight
On my face a dark smear.

Listen with your heart, not your head for a change
I started to argue and then out it came!
A hilarious laugh that brought tears to my eyes
I didn't take myself seriously, as this ditty implies!!

"IF"

If I could paint a landscape
It would contain Florida's brilliant skies
If I could paint a moonbeam
You'd be there by my side.

If I could paint the winds
Wafting sweetly through the trees
If I could paint the love of God
Your face is what I'd see

If I could paint the lavender's scent
What tranquility it would bring
If I could paint a lullaby
Oh, the lovely music it would sing

I surely would, if I could
But there is nothing more
He has done it for us
Just open your front door.

NOTES

How has the Lord reflected Himself through these verses?

1.

2.

PARADISE

Shadows falling here and there

As the sun warmly enshrines a pirouette

Playing a gentle dance only a

Ballerina can understand

Flowers moving in graceful obedience

To the shifting of the winds

Cooing of turtle doves encase the

Morning horizon

Lights aglow, twinkling

Honoring the rising darkness

Noises of the birds awakening to

Yet a new experience

Yes, another beautiful day in paradise.

MOM

(This was written by my daughter, Deborah Gile)

Rock a bye baby and similar songs.
Mother would teach us as we grew along.
The years went fast and the heartaches were few,
No matter the issue a hug from mom
would always do.

Jumping fences and digging in ditches,
Scraped knees, Band-Aids and grown up wishes.
Active young boys, girls in pretty dresses,
Mom always taught us to clean up our messes.

Be nice and kind and lend a helping hand,
Achievements are greater when united we stand.
Reminders to grab your coat while she made PB&J,
She'd help with our homework at the end of each day.

Cars lined up like an alliance
At swim meets she'd cheer and always be beside us.
Cooking and cleaning and all things recreational,
Clipping coupons for shopping, now
that was sensational!

In troubled times, Mom was always a welcomed
invasion, a friend beside us in our most scary
situations. She listened; she loved, and
reminded us to be true,
And this Mother's Day, I'm so grateful for you.

DAY OF THE LORD

The heavens emptied itself of its vestments.

The stars refused to shine.

An aura of holiness permeated the air

Hallelujah!! The Day of the Lord is nigh.

The trumpet blast is breaking forth

Below, the firmament does quake

Calliopes of people are anxiously aware

The Day of the Lord is taking place!!

Then through the veil of clouds we see Him

Standing, suspended in time

Our Savior, our Lover coming home as foretold

To receive His all worshipping Bride!!

This will happen, for there is no doubt

Just make sure you are not the one *left* out!!

CLOCKS

We all stand before God naked
Stripped of all our clothes
Our souls are barren in His sight
Why? This is the way He chose.

We are not to question our Father
Don't ask why, where or when
He has a reason that will better our lives
Though we can't see it just then.

He has ordained our life and
He also knows the end
We can't understand the trials
No, not just then.

So pray to the Father
And in faith, look to the Rock
Knowing that when the darkness lifts
There will be no need for clocks!!

GOOD BYE

There is never a right time to say GOOD BYE

I think "Au revoir" sounds better

"Auf Wiedersehen" has the same connotation

But I prefer "See you later."

So, my friend, though we must part

In this memory we will be together forever!!

NOTES

How has the Lord reflected Himself through these verses?

1.

2.

REFLECTIONS OF HIM

MEDITATIONS

(Note paper available at the back of book)

ANNIVERSARY

I had something exciting happen a few days ago. It all started on the day of my 55th anniversary, the second since the Lord called my hubby home. As you can expect, I was feeling lonely when all of a sudden the phone rang. A delivery man was at my front door. I hurriedly opened to a man holding the most beautiful floral arrangement I had seen. My first words were "I wonder what I did." The man secretly chuckled and replied "It must have been something special to receive these beautiful flowers." I thanked him and brought the arrangement inside. Who could this be from?

Excitedly, I opened the card!! "Happy anniversary...We love you." I was shocked. The children had never done anything like this before. I did a "check list" in my mind trying to figure out what I had done to deserve this. The Lord took that moment to teach yet another lesson, "Now you can understand how special it feels, how loved, realizing that you had to do nothing to earn this, but they love you for who you are!! That is what I want too - people who will praise and honor me not only for the blessings or answered prayer but just because they LOVE ME!!"

Heavenly Father allow us to become so immersed in You that we realize **You are the biggest and most important GIFT!!**

CHRISTMAS OF 2017

This is the wonderful Christmas season of 2017. I can't believe this year is almost over. I am happy to announce that I have the answer to a question that has been bothering me. Please let me explain what I mean.

Two days ago I was driving home from a Christmas party when the Lord started speaking to me. Wait a minute – That's not exactly how it happened. Okay now for the revised edition of my story – Two days ago I was at a Christmas party where we shared Christmas cards and wrote an encouraging word on them. Nice way to start the New Year.

We didn't know which card we were going to receive but we were certain that the Lord would make sure we each got the right one. My card stated that the year 2018 was the year that the Lord was going to show me how I fit into His Plan. I was excited as I had been reading many books on this exact theme but no direct answer had been found.

On my way home I decided to ask the Lord to give me the answer a little early?? I would have never guessed what would transpire next. *"Let your light so shine among men that they may see your good deeds and glorify your Father which is in Heaven." "Let your life be hid in God,"* was His reply!! It was so clear, so easy that I had missed it completely. My Father doesn't just want my service but He wants ALL of me!!

As I was meditating, this picture of a Christmas gift all wrapped up with a pretty red bow flashed across my mind. "We have this treasure in earthen vessels." To the world we are their Christmas present and if they see our good works they will be drawn to look inside the vessel to the Treasure. To our Heavenly Father we are to be the tissue paper inside the box … so thin that He can see Jesus being created and then spread into all areas of our lives. **Thank you Father for this honor and place in Your Plan. Merry Christmas!!**

BOUQUET OF WEEDS

My grandmother and then my mother had a tradition called "Sunday Dinners" with the whole family there to enjoy the meal and each other also. This tradition had started way back in the 1940's with my grandmother's house the central theme of each meeting. My Granny passed away in 1977 and my mother took up the tradition and had the Sunday meals at her home with all invited. My dear mother went to be with the Lord in 2005 so I decided that the baton was passed to me and I kept up the dinners at my house. After dinner my granddaughters, 3 and 2, asked if they could walk around the block with their dads as chaperones.

When they came home, the door opened and, very quickly, I heard "Grandma close your eyes and reach out our hand." As I obeyed, I felt something very soft in my palm. When I opened my natural eyes, the Lord opened my spiritual eyes at the same time. In my hand was a clump of dandelions. The girls thought they were beautiful flowers when they were just the opposite. As I stared at the dandelions they became the most beautiful bouquet because my girls had picked them especially for me. At the same time the Lord spoke to my heart, **"That is how I feel when you give me your sins. I make beauty out of the ashes of your life. The clump of sin you offer me becomes the most beautiful bouquet of love."**

DECISION

I recently went through a situation that I felt was truly unfair. Has that ever happened to you? Something had occurred that seemed unjust yet you were constrained by the Lord not to talk about it or to defend yourself? Yep, that's what I mean. I decided to talk to the Lord on this one and, during my tantrum, I confess that I used words not in my usual vocabulary. It didn't bother the Lord one bit.

First, as always, He comforted me and then asked a question, "You really want them to get what they deserve, don't you? Remember that if I give them what they deserve I will also have to give you what you deserve for I am a Just and Holy God!!" Whoops! Never thought of that Lord! "You want to see them get their "reward" but remember, if you do see it then you lose yours in heaven. Every path you walk and overcome you receive a jewel in your crown but if you see it here, you lose it there. What do you want Me to do?"

"*Bless them*" was all I could say!!

DINNER PARTY

One day a very wealthy man decided he would have a dinner party. He called his butler and told him about the event. The man wanted not just a dinner party; he wanted a very special kind of dinner with seven courses. He explained that at each course he needed a special glass. The first will be the champagne toast and he needed the champagne glasses. The second, a water glass was needed. The third, a beer mug and etc.......The final course was to have been dessert so a coffee mug was needed. When the time came for the dinner and everyone was seated in their respective places, the host stood and gave directions to the group gathered. "During this dinner we will be using a different glass for every course and it will be your job to remember that at the count of 3 we will then, all together, throw our glasses and break them. After each course we will do the same." The guests looked at each other in surprise. They were each thinking "He really must be rich if he can use a different container for each course and then BREAK it!!

Does that sound familiar? It should because it is a picture of the Lord and what he does to all His sons!! There is a scripture **"He chastens all those he calls sons."**

He really does!! Have you been standing and all of a sudden you start crying? Someone asked me why I was crying and I couldn't tell him then. I know why now. WE are all to be like those glasses at the dinner party. Fit for the Masters use but then broken and reshaped for the next time He needs us. It was during this breaking process that I was crying and didn't know why. **If you want a tender and softened heart for His use you will find that breaking is a process that happens again and again until we see Him at the gates. See you there!!**

END DAYS

Can you feel the tensions in the atmosphere? It seems to me all creation is getting ready for something BIG. You and I both know what that means. Scripture describes the "end days" as filled with diverse warnings like we have never seen before. Remember the earthquake in Virginia that "rocked" even the buildings in Manhattan? Some of our American landmarks were jolted and chipped!! The earthquake measured 5.9 on the Richter Scale; the hurricanes that have hit Florida in the past 15 years; the dams breaking in New Orleans? All these are but warnings of the great judgment that will soon take place.

Are you ready? This is a question I ask myself almost daily. The closer we get to the "end of the age" the fiercer the temptations will be, the stronger our "flesh" will want to be victor. We must be ready for this onslaught. If we have not made Jesus and His Word the fundamentals which we live by, we won't make it through. I need His help every day just to be able to prepare myself for what is ahead. The earth is being prepared!! *Are you?*

FRIENDS

This morning it occurred to me that love and being loved in return has both its up and downs. I was thinking about my mother and the good times she and I had. I can remember that when everything and everyone else seemed to leave, my mother was always there. Of course this led me to the Cross and how Jesus was left. All His friends abandoned Him and you hear nothing about His brothers and sisters, so you can assume that the only people there were John the Beloved and His mother.

There was a time in my life when I was very sick. I had a closed head injury and it left me with grand mal epilepsy. Needless to say, everyone was afraid to be with me as I might have a seizure so, little by little, my friends left me. I can't remember much about that period but what I can remember is my mother standing over me and just sobbing!! I knew that she would have gladly switched places with me. That's a mother's love!! Let's take that a step further and compare our earthly mother's love to that of Jesus. I was reading Isaiah 58:8:" The chastisement for our peace was upon Him, and by His stripes we are healed." Jesus did what every mother would do to protect her loved ones. Jesus is our Protector, Savior, Lord, Healer and most importantly our Best Friend!!

FUTURE

We all agree that no one knows what the future holds but I find myself trying to plan for it anyway. Have you ever found yourself hoping that it would not rain during the next week so you can have a picnic outside with the family? Maybe you had decided to have a small private ceremony of some kind on Sept 22? Or maybe you made plans with friends for dinner and cards next weekend? We don't realize but we are planning our own futures when, if we were asked, we would readily agree that only God knows!!

How silly we humans are and how many smiles we must bring to His Face as he sees us scurrying around like tiny ants in the "picnic" we call life. I just pray our Heavenly Father will help us slow down so that we don't miss any more of His blessings. When we are so concentrated on the future, I feel we are surely missing out on His **Best today!!**

GIFT OF TODAY

The inky blackness has given way to an effervescent orb exploding on the horizon shedding itself in a rainbow of light and color on all it touches. Another beautiful day in "paradise." Taking in its beauty, I am astounded at the myriad of emotions being felt all at once. Truly, thankfulness for another breath, another minute, another hour. At the same time trepidation at what might be around the next corner that I will, once more, have to face. I must learn that the past is over, behind me. The future is not yet and may never come to fruition. All I have of any significant value is the "now."

My energies must be consecrated to the moments I have, trying as best I can to make this day a little easier for those around me. Not revisiting anger, bitterness or jealousy for the things that were; not worrying how to face the next situation that will or will not pass my way; but attending to the present. The past is like a door swinging open but for a moment then shutting forever. The future is likened to the butterfly that may or may not land in our backyards.

Lord, help me to wisely use your gift of TODAY.

GIFTS

Each one of us has been given special and unique talents that are suited for our personality, interests, passions, etc. I can remember a time years ago when the Lord told me He would fill my hands with His Wisdom. When it didn't happen, in what I thought was a sufficient amount of time. I decided to try it MY way. Sound familiar?

It now is 45 years later and I must confess that I still am waiting. Or am I? That's a question we all have to answer each day. As the months turn into years and the years turn into decades, I believe that we understand we are on a journey. To continue on this "journey" we must have a path or way that leads us to our goal. You also need a way out if something bad befalls you. "I am the Way to Salvation and I am also the way out of any dangerous, scary situation. All you need do is call on My Name and I hear and I'll answer. Never think that I have forgotten your request only that there is a time for the answer and it may not be now. **Never fear I keep My Promises"!!**

LORD REIGNS

I am happy to report that the Lord Jesus still reigns no matter what temptation you are going through. Last week I wrote down my thoughts as I was deep in a situation where even the merest thought of what my soul craved sickened me. They were so out of line with the Word of God I was ashamed to even admit them. Does this sound familiar? Needless to say, I prayed with no results. Many of my experiences with God are so vivid that a person would have to be "oblivious" to miss His Voice, then other times, usually times of temptation, I hear nothing. The silence just drones on and on.

Little by little a scripture started to form "There is nothing hidden that shall not be revealed." The Lord answers us in many different ways. My answer now came through my daughter. My granddaughter, 11, was having a problem. She had been told not to mention something to her mother. Thankfully, Rachael didn't listen. It was during the answer from my daughter that the Lord revealed MY answer. "If someone tells you to keep a "secret" from your parent, that is a warning sign. There should never be anything you can't be candid about. Who loves you and is more interested than your parents? How true!! I looked my situation right in the "eye" and made an appointment to clear it up once and for all. Sometimes we have to humble ourselves and discuss with the other party involved. This is what I did! That one discussion took care of all my wakeful nights. We parted friends and I am still thanking the Lord for his great Wisdom. **If you feel a need to hide something remember He is Light and where He is darkness (sin has to flee).**

MOTHER'S DAY

Do you remember the family photo albums? I sure do!! My aunt used to take pictures of everything that happened to me and my children and then, years later, we would all sit down after dinner and take out the "Family "book. The albums have become pictures we save on our cell phones now but the important thing is that we still savor our lives and memorialize them with pictures. I have said all this because of a situation that must have been stored way in the back of my mind being saved for a time such as now.

It took place May 1976 (before some of you were even born). My daughter invited me to a Mother's Day banquet at her church. The dinner was great and then a special guest appeared. The woman was an artist and she had brought her easel and special paper along with charcoal pens. She was very talented and the picture she drew was lovely. It was a landscape drawing in black and white. She said not a word but just kept drawing. When she was finished she turned a light on the picture and the landscape illuminated with color!! I couldn't believe it. All the drawing needed was a special light and the stark white paper became vivid with color!! Before me was a picture, in the natural, of what the Lord, spiritually, had done to my life. The boring existence I had been living became illuminated with His Presence and new Life was brought to me. If you know the Lord as your personal Savior that is what happened to you too. **If not, today is the day of salvation.**

MOM

The aged woman with gnarled knuckles and snow white hair was working intently on her craft. As her fingers stumbled, stopped, then started yet again to decipher her crocheting, I paused in reverie. I can remember those arthritic appendages in their youth as they lay on my forehead checking for a fever. Her hands were beautiful with nails caressed in a deep scarlet paint. So soft, so full of love and comfort, yet how insignificant it all seemed to me then. I stand here as an adult and wonder why Mom was taken from me just when I could finally appreciate her true beauty inside and out!

I sigh as I realize I am looking into the DVD of my mind, watching a rerun, being played out before me. Guess it's time to finish the blanket I am crocheting!!

NAMES

"Jesus, name above all names, Beautiful Savior, Glorious Lord." Just sat down and those words started singing in my spirit. How wonderful He is and how lucky we are to have such a Friend. Each day some new situation faces us and we need the Character of Christ to help us overcome. Sometimes we need His humility; other times we need His Courage. When our enemies are afflicting us we need His Love. When we are sick, we need His healing ... and on it goes. I pray that you know him in all His different aspects for He knows you in all of yours!

QUANTITY VS QUALITY

It has been a long time in between visits but I refuse to give you my own opinion and thoughts. Why? Unfortunately, I don't have the Words of Life, only He does. So only He can speak to your heart and change your life not me, as much as I would like to think that I could. Enough said!! As I was awakening from sleep, the thought crossed my not-yet-awakened brain "Quality or Quantity." As I started to reflect on that thought the Lord started showing me why every once in a while my "uh-oh" meter starts buzzing when I hear "There were 80 people in church Sunday" or "We need to start more programs so more people will come to church."

Are we looking for quantity in numbers or is there something more important that we should be focusing on? A good example was the 2016 presidential race. I have never seen so many looking to become president but is the number of men/women vying for the job important or is the quality of their message the important thing? I pray when the service in your church wherever that may be, is ended that you walk out the doors with more of Jesus than you came in with. The Lord left the 99 for the 1 and I am praying that all of us will **leave the numbers behind** and concentrate on Him.

ROUTINE

This morning began like every other. I have started a regimen of swimming, water aerobics and walking. I know this "plan of action" is good, but ... Isn't that always the way, everything that's good for us can't be enjoyed? Oh, I have tried but I just can't. Every time I walk with the TV video and she says, "Now doesn't that feel good"? I cringe a little more.

During my morning scripture reading a question flew into my mind... "Do you preach the Word with your mouth, or with your life, or with both?" That took me by surprise!! I had never thought about it, but since He brought up the subject, I knew I had to look at it! Many times, at least in my world, I tend to ignore the subjects I don't want to deal with. This would NOT be one of those times, I could just tell!!

Faithless as I am, the Lord still LOVES me. I still belong to Him. So do you. I think this question comes to us encouraging us to follow Him closer. Just when we think we have it all down "pat" He adds another "street" to our journey home. **Without a backward glance, keeping your eyes on the Prize ... Have a blessed day.**

SUMMERTIME

I have had a most interesting summer. Many ups and downs but I am happy to report God came through every time. I don't mean that I got all the answers I was after but during the times of disappointment, the Lord taught me many lessons and spiritually I am in a lot better shape than before. My pockets aren't, but … it was during one of those hard and disappointing times that I woke up one morning with this question on my heart. "Dear Lord use me as a servant? Talk to me as a Friend? Love me like a little child?" I had the head knowledge but my heart was asking why????

Three days later I awoke with a prayer on my heart. "Dear Lord thank you for using me as your servant, talking to me as a friend, and loving me like YOUR little child." What had happened? My questions from three days before had turned into a beautiful statement coming from the depths of my heart. Only our wonderful Savior can make beauty from ashes, give the oil of joy for mourning and garments of praise for our spirit of heaviness!!

SUNFLOWER

It must be 45 years ago. One day, during my private devotions, the Lord called me His sunflower. I didn't really understand the importance of that statement. I didn't know much but I did know that there had to be a something special about a sunflower and Jesus was inviting me to come to His table of Learning. Join me?

I started out by reading about the flower. First importance - the blossom always keeps its face towards the sun. During the nighttime, the blossom sleeps, bending its stalk and when the sun shines, up come its beautiful head to welcome in the splendor of a new day. What a picture!! If we could attain that!!

Secondly, as the sunflowers wait expectantly for the wedding of summer to fall, the blossoms that were not harvested are left to mature. When the blossoms have reached their maturity, they bow their heads and all the seeds that make up the "brown" middle section fall, planting and distributing the seeds into fertile soil. What a beautiful picture this is of a WORKER for you, Jesus.

Lastly, the sunflower not only keeps its face to the sun, but follows the sun by turning on its stalk. How many times I have tried to do that, follow the Lord and have failed miserably. Yet, all I had to do was, like the bloom of the sunflower, just sit in His Presence and **BE** for Him!!

SYMPHONY

My son and I were given tickets to see the symphony. Our tickets were for seats in the back but the usher escorted us to the front instead. The Lord is so good He places you right where He wants. Anyway, the symphony was wonderful but my attention stayed on the conductor. I was so enthralled watching his arm move, the baton showing each musical section when to play, seeing a picture of how the Father just orchestrates our world. I was brought up short when my eye happened to pick up on the violin section.

All of a sudden they stopped playing and took their instruments and put them under their right arms. With their eyes always on the conductor, they waited patiently until his baton signaled and they started playing again. It was at that time the Lord spoke to my heart and said, "Under My Wing shall you learn to trust." When I arrived home I went on the internet to find out why the violinists placed their violins under their arms. The answer just about knocked my socks off!! The violinists were keeping the strings warm so that, when they played again, the strings would not be cold and break. Jesus keeps us under His Wing until He is ready to send us out in the cold world again for His use!! The words **"Play on your instrument, your instrument of worship"** rang through my heart.

TEMPTATION

As ministers of the gospel, we all have certain responsibilities, none more important than living what we speak. Unfortunately, that is often a goal we cannot attain to. I have wondered, more than once, why that is…Now I am experiencing first hand. Have you even been in a situation that, years or months before, you would have been abhorred if someone even suggested that it would become a temptation? Well guess what!! Here I am. I would never have believed it but I am right in the middle of that now. I have weighed the good against the bad and sin is always heavier. I guess that's why Jesus calls it a BURDEN!

I am sharing this because confession is good for the soul, mine right now, and also to make you aware that temptation strikes us all, different ways at different times, to be sure, but we must all overcome every day. My only survival method is Jesus and His love for me. I remember how devastated Peter was when he denied His Lord. Jesus loves us so much that He gave up His Life. **Can we do less?**

TIME 'FLYS'

Years fly by! Growing up I can remember that cliché coming from my mother. I always agreed but somewhere deep inside I thought, "she must be getting older!" Now I know how RIGHT mother was. Isn't it strange how your mother becomes so wise so FAST!! Seems like yesterday I knew mother didn't have all the answers. Today I can say, with all honesty, she really was RIGHT about so many things I wanted her to be WRONG about. That protective, nurturing love that I tried so hard to get free of now looks like a "safe port." I am just rattling on... but didn't Jesus tell us not to forget from whence we had come? I lost mother about 14 years ago. She sure was a gem. My loss is truly heaven's gain. I envy mom. She can sit down with Jesus and touch His lovely Face any time she wants. Mom can sing praises (and on key too)!! The best part, for me, will be the day when I see Mom along with a crowd of friends and relatives, waiting and cheering for me as I walk in the Gates!! **What a day that will be!!**

THE CURTAIN

My husband heard a giant thud and went into the bedroom to find that our curtain over the big window had fallen. Secretly I was glad because I wanted to get something new but, a few days later I decided to go visit my neighbor and was surprised to see that she was getting new blinds. I have always liked the swag she had so I asked her if I could use it in my bedroom, never dreaming what I was asking for! It looked so easy! Just take the material and throw it over the rod and bingo you are done. As I was leaving my neighbor said, "Good luck putting it up. I worked for 3 weeks to get it the way I wanted." I couldn't believe it. It looked so simple. When I was done I asked Kathy to come over and check it out. After she was through with her examination she told me that her daughter was coming down and could just give the swag the last finishing touches it needed.

What happened next was so simple yet complex at the same time. Her daughter came over and touched the material here and there and all of a sudden the swag billowed full!! It was beautiful!! It was then that I remembered the song "He **Touched** Me."

Do you remember the first time He **touched** you? The scripture in Genesis takes on a new meaning now. The Lord took dirt and breathed into it and it became a living soul. He **touched** the dirt and made it live, and hopefully, he has **touched** you and you have experienced His life in you. If not, there is no better time than right now!!

VICTORIOUS DEFEAT

"For everything there is a season under the heavens" ... The only problem with that is my timing and His timing don't have the same agenda ... Life is a losing battle. I hope or it should be. We were not intended nor created to be the saviors of each and every situation. Now comes the hard part – <u>easy to say, hard to live</u>. "The spirit is willing but the flesh is weak." I understand with every passing day the meaning of Paul's words when he said, "Oh wretched man that I am." I try so hard to do right, to walk the Christian walk, but it just doesn't compute!! All my good works, thoughts and intentions just bottom out!!

Each of us has the SAME story to write. Different situations but the ending is never unique. Same old stuff...we can't do it ourselves. Many different experiences leading to the same finish line with the same results – JESUS in charge. Why I can't get that through to my flesh, I don't know. Maybe that is why life is called a "journey."

I pray that today you and I will wake up in victorious defeat (knowing that in us there is no good thing but in Him dwells every good gift). Understanding that we can do nothing to affect change only His **Victory** takes us to the prize....See you there!!

WATER AND THE WORD

We recently came back to our winter home. It really is paradise here. Even when it's cool, like today, it is still 71 degrees. I call my daughters in Michigan and invariably we get to talking about the weather. I kind of chuckle to myself as I think of the old days when my mother used to call me from down here.

Yesterday, I was in the pool doing my laps. When I finished, I decided to just float for a while, as I was tired. I closed my eyes and just drifted on top of the water. When I opened my eyes, I was at the deep end. I had started in the shallow end but the water had buoyed me to the deep end without having to exert myself one bit.

Then I saw the picture the Lord had been painting. If our natural water can buoy us and keep us afloat even in dangerous depths, how **much more can our Lord Jesus, who is the Water of the Word, keep and protect!!**

WINTER HOME

I have been in Florida, my winter home, for one week. The weather is terrific, in the low 80's. Yesterday I was finishing my laps in the pool and drying off. "And who do <u>you</u> say that I am"? Came through loud and clear!!

I have to confess that, at first I was a little taken aback. The Lord knows my heart, and I thought we were good friends and then, this!

The more I meditated on His question the more I realized that it was not just a one-time question and answer. Forty-five years ago I answered it, but now I see that I have to answer this again each day. **He is asking you the same question. Have a blessed day!!**

NOTES

How has the Lord reflected Himself through these thoughts?

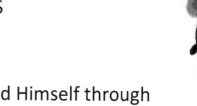

NOTES

How has the Lord reflected Himself through these thoughts?

NOTES

How has the Lord reflected Himself through
these thoughts?

NOTES

How has the Lord reflected Himself through these thoughts?

NOTES

How has the Lord reflected Himself through these thoughts?

THE END

I must confess that this has been harder than I thought. Writing down my ideas and thoughts are the easiest part of the process. I pray that you have been reading through this book and have been blessed. I realize that my reflections are only a taste of what the Lord has waiting for all those that are seeking a closer and more intimate relationship with Him. There is so much more waiting for us. I'm on my way.

Barbara De Croix

ACKNOWLEDGEMENTS

I would like to thank Kenneth Turner Blackshaw for his expertise, long hours and editing on this writing without which this book could not have been published. Also thanks to Pastor Gary Clark, Fellowship Church, for his obedience and encouragement (push) to start writing.

Thanks go to Hannah Wilson (my grand daughter) for the lovely borders used in this book.

Hats off to my son Rick DeCroix, Streamline Films, for taking hours from his busy schedule to help edit my final copy.

Lastly, I want to thank my family and friends for putting up with me through this process.

If you have comments, send them to:

signlady43@gmail.com

Made in the USA
Columbia, SC
26 May 2019